Hoberman, Mary
A Little Book of
Little Beast.

Book of Little Beasts

Pictures by

PETER PARNALL

SIMON AND SCHUSTER · NEW YORK

A Little Book
of Little Beasts

MARY ANN HOBERMAN

To Meg

Text copyright © 1973 by Mary Ann Hoberman
Illustrations copyright © 1973 by Peter Parnall
All rights reserved
including the right of reproduction
in whole or in part in any form
Published by Simon and Schuster, Children's Book Division
Rockefeller Center, 630 Fifth Avenue
New York, New York 10020

First Printing

SBN 671-65203-6 Reinforced Edition
Library of Congress Catalog Card Number: 72-88404
Manufactured in the United States of America
Designed by Jack Jaget

Contents

Little Beasts   6

How Many?   8

Mole   12

Opossum   16

Frog   18

Chipmunk   20

Worm   22

Who Am I? (I)   24

Snake   25

Mouse   26

Birdsongsingsong   30

Raccoon   32

Question   34

Who Am I? (II)   36

Squirrel   38

Shrew   40

Rabbit   44

Muskrat   46

Vice Versa Verse   48

A Little Book of Little Beasts

Little beasts like little books
>> To peek in
>> To play in.
Little beasts like little books
>> To be in
>> To stay in.
Big books make them feel so small
Big books aren't right at all
Little books are what they prize
Little books are just their size
>> Warm and cozy
>> Snug and tight
>> Fitting absolutely right.
Little books are what they need
And here is one for you to read.

Jessica

How Many?

A mother skunk all black and white
Leads her babies down the street
    Pitter patter
    Pitter patter
    Pitter patter
    TWENTY feet.

Off they toddle slow and steady
Making tiny twitter cries
    Flitter flutter
    Flitter flutter
    Flitter flutter
    TEN small eyes.

Nose to tail-tip in procession
Single-file the family trails
    Flippy floppy
    Flippy floppy
    Flippy floppy
    FIVE long tails.

9

Up the street a dog comes barking,
Sees the strangers, leaps pell-mell . . .
    Ickle pickle
    Ickle pickle
    Ickle pickle
    ONE BIG SMELL!

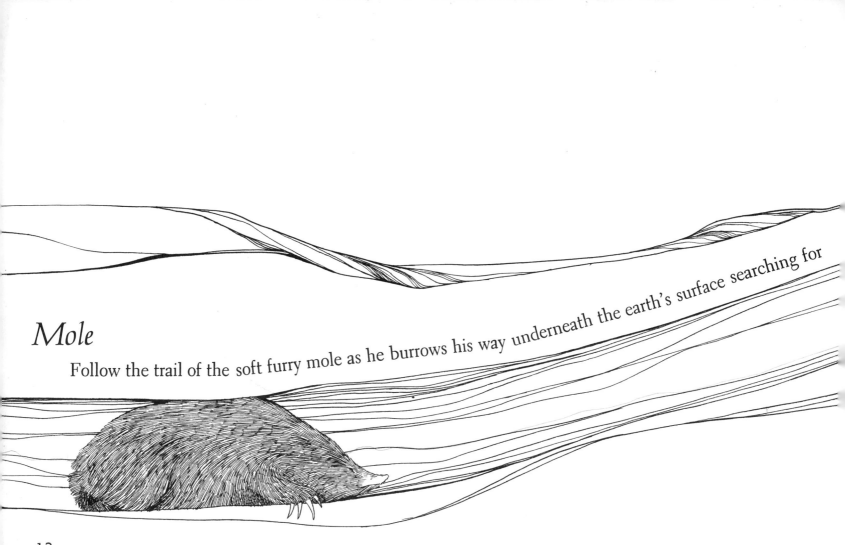

Mole

Follow the trail of the soft furry mole as he burrows his way underneath the earth's surface searching for

12

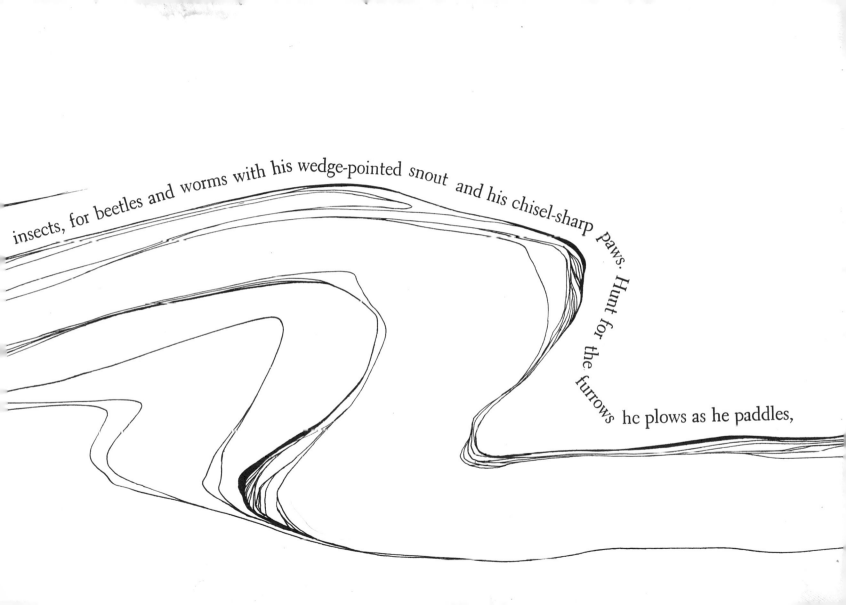

insects, for beetles and worms with his wedge-pointed snout and his chisel-sharp paws. Hunt for the furrows he plows as he paddles,

forced to keep feeding his never-stilled hunger. Look for the humps and the bumps and the lumps that

14

he strews out behind him . . . and then go and find him.

Opossum

O possum, I followed
Your starfooted track.
      Your babies were hiding
      Inside of your sac.

O possum, I saw you
Aprowl in the black.
      Your babies were riding
      Astride on your back.

O possum, I found you
Asleep near a shack.
      Your babies had left you.
      Alas and alack!

Frog

Pollywiggle
Pollywog
Tadpole
Bullfrog
Leaps on
Long legs
Jug-o-rum
Jelly eggs
Sticky tongue
Tricks flies
Spied by
Flicker eyes

Wet skin
Cold blood
Squats in
Mucky mud
Leaps on
Long legs
Jug-o-rum
Jelly eggs
Laid in
Wet bog. . . .
Pollywiggle
Pollywog.

Chipmunk

Chipmunk,
Do not be afraid.
Though you are so small and frail,
You can vanish from the spot
In the flicker of a tail.
Or, if it's too late to flee,
In your autumn-colored pelt
You can, like a pod or leaf,
Deep into the shadows melt.

Worm

Squiggly wiggly wriggly *jiggly* ziggly higgly piggly worm watch it

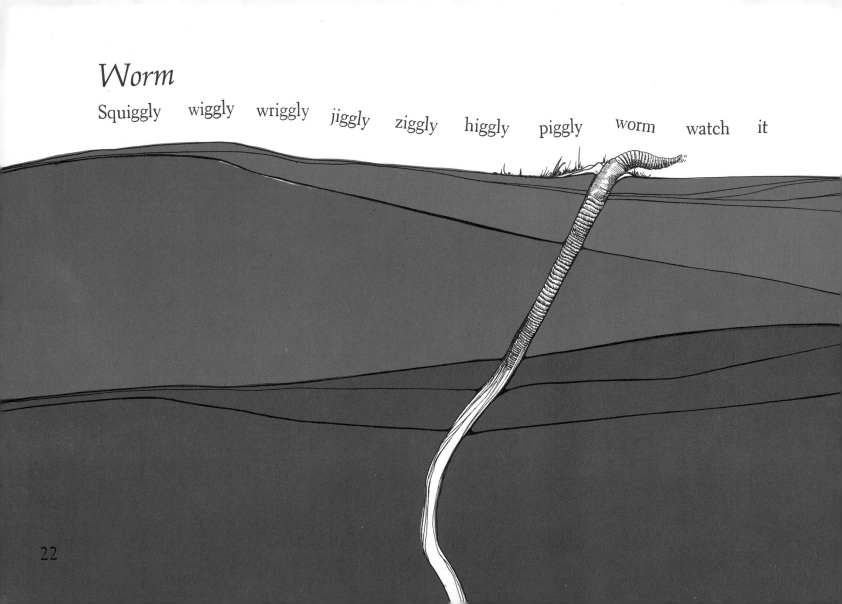

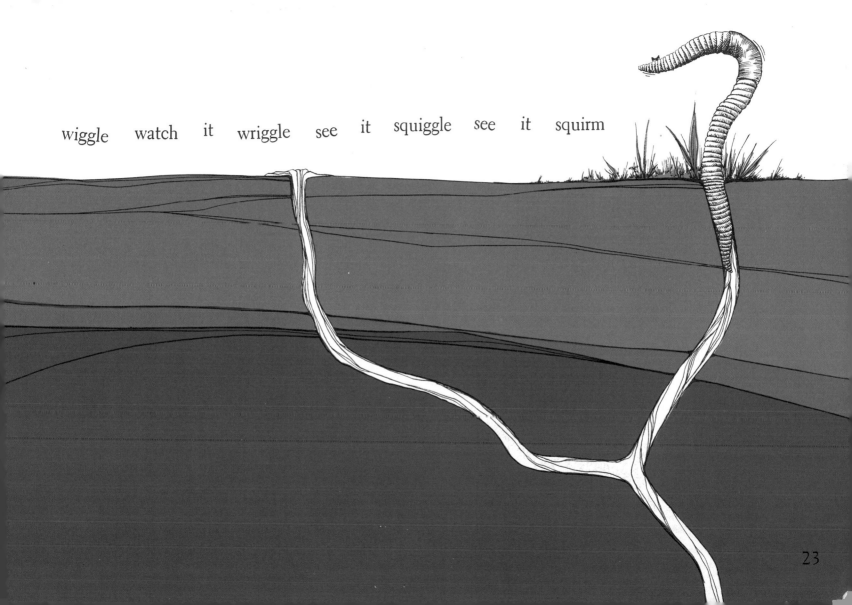

wiggle   watch it wriggle   see it squiggle   see it squirm

23

Who Am I? (I)

A big buzz
In a little fuzz.

Snake

A snake will sometimes slither by
Straight and skinny as an I.
It's sometimes shaped just like an S
Or curved, like C, a little less.
Have you ever tried to get
Yourself into the alphabet?

Mouse

Dear little
Mere little
Merry little
Meadow mouse
    Where do you live? Where do you live?
In a mole's hole
Bird's nest
Hollow of a hickory
    That's where I live. That's where I live.

Dear little
Mere little
Merry little
Meadow mouse
    What do you do? What do you do?
Hunt for food and
Care for my babies
    That's what I do. That's what I do.

28

Dear little
Mere little
Merry little
Meadow mouse
      What do you eat? What do you eat?

Roots and
Seeds and
Nuts and
Insects
      That's what I eat. That's what I eat.

Dear little
Mere little
Merry little
Meadow mouse
      What do you fear? What do you fear?
Every kind of stranger
Every kind of danger
      That's what I fear. That's what I fear.

Dear little
Mere little
Merry little
Meadow mouse
      What do you love? What do you love?
Running and
Racing and
Chasing round in circles
      That's what I love. That's what I love.

Birdsongsingsong

birds
need
bird
seed
bird
seed
feeds
birds
birds
sing
bird
song
songs
with
bird
words

birds
fly
sky
high
dive
deep
fly
birds
twilight
ends
flight
good
night
sleep
birds

Raccoon

Crash goes the trashcan! Clatter and clacket!
What in the world can be making that racket?
I hurry to look by the light of the moon,
And what do I find? Why, a fine fat raccoon!
All through the garden the garbage he's strewn,
And he's eating his supper, that robber raccoon,
Eating so nicely without fork or spoon,
Why, his manners are perfect, that thieving raccoon!
And wasn't he smart to discover that pail?
And wasn't he smart to uncover that pail?
And isn't he lucky he won't go to jail
For stealing his dinner and making a mess
For me to clean up in the morning, I guess,
While he, the old pirate, abundantly fed,
Curls up in a ball fast asleep in his bed.

Question

— Did you ever ever ever think
That every ant you've ever seen
Must be a princess or a prince
Because its mother is a queen?

"Remember me!"
Buzzed the bee.
"I am also
Royalty."

Who Am I? (II)

No matter where I travel,
No matter where I roam,
No matter where I find myself,
I always am at home.

Sniffed the snail
In its shell,
"This fact is true
Of me as well."

37

Squirrel

Gray squirrel
        Small beast,
Storing up a winter's feast,
Hides a hundred nuts at least.

Nook and cranny stocked with seed
Tucked away for winter's need.
Acorns stuck in hole and crack.
Will he ever get them back?

When the snow is piled up high
And the year is at December,
Can he really still remember
Where he hid them in September?

I have watched him from my window
And he always seems to know
Where the food he hid is waiting
Buried deep beneath the snow.

And I wonder
        (Do you wonder?)
How he knows where he must go.

39

Shrew

The shrew is so busy she makes me quite dizzy she always is running she never is still
Her appetite rules her she always is hungry she always is hunting to capture her fill

Of spiders and centipedes earthworms and crickets garden snakes meadow mice grasshoppers snails
With her long pointed snout she is poking them out as she scampers about along tunnels and trails

She never slows down like a sensible animal even in winter she dashes around
Chasing and racing through snowdrifts and hollows while common-sense creatures are snug underground
But her vigorous life doesn't last the way theirs do she lives and she dies within five hundred days
Sniffing and searching through summer and winter she wears herself out with her hard-working ways

Until one dark evening on frost-coated stubble while out on an errand she stumbles and drops
And her motor runs down

It gets lower and lower

Goes slower and slower

And finally

Stops

Rabbit

A rabbit
bit
A little bit
An itty bitty
Little bit of beet.
Then bit
By bit
He bit
Because he liked the taste of it.
But when he bit
A wee bit more,
It was more bitter than before.
"This beet is bitter!"
Rabbit cried.
"I feel a bit unwell inside!"
But when he bit
Another bite, that bit of beet
Seemed quite all right.
Besides when all is said and done,
Better bitter beet than none.

45

Muskrat

At dusk the muskrat quits his den
And rises up to take a swim.
He paddles with his webbed feet.
Silver ripples follow him.
He looks and listens as he glides
Across the shadows and beyond;
And if he sees you watching him,
He vanishes into the pond.

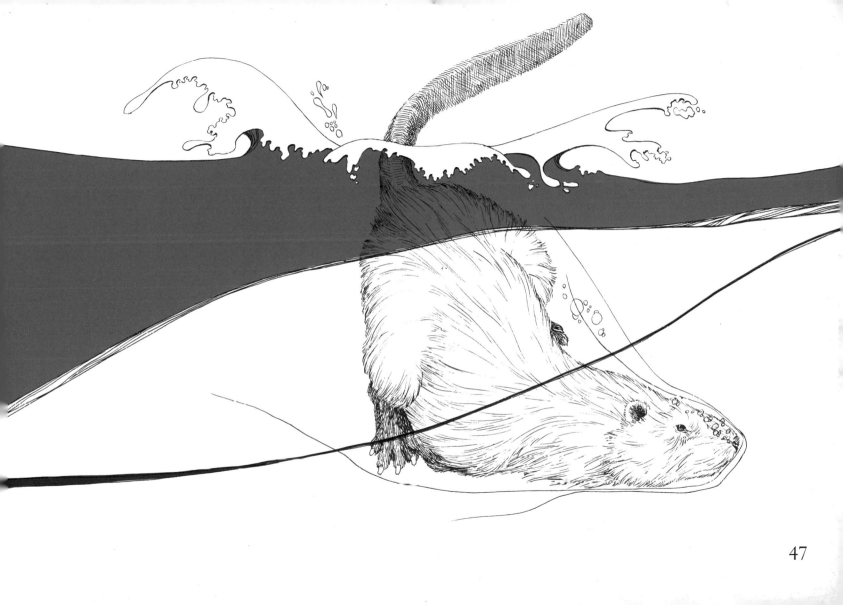

Vice Versa Verse

A hedgehog lives in hedges
A porcupine in pines
        Do you believe what I just said?
        Do you believe the sky is red
        Or that I'm standing on my head?
Or am I only fooling?

A porcupine's a porky pig
A hedgehog is a hog
        Do you believe what I just said?
        Do you believe my name is Fred
        Or that the world is gingerbread?
Or am I only fooling?

A porcupine and hedgehog
Are really just the same
        Do you believe what I just said?
        Do you believe what you just read?
        Or will you look it up instead
And find out if I'm fooling?